Poisoned By Love.
Still Thirsty.

A Reality So Intense, Only Poetry Could Tell

Pranav Sood

Copyright © Pranav Sood
All Rights Reserved.

This book has been self-published with all reasonable efforts taken to make the material error-free by the author. No part of this book shall be used, reproduced in any manner whatsoever without written permission from the author, except in the case of brief quotations embodied in critical articles and reviews.

The Author of this book is solely responsible and liable for its content including but not limited to the views, representations, descriptions, statements, information, opinions, and references ["Content"]. The Content of this book shall not constitute or be construed or deemed to reflect the opinion or expression of the Publisher or Editor. Neither the Publisher nor Editor endorse or approve the Content of this book or guarantee the reliability, accuracy, or completeness of the Content published herein and do not make any representations or warranties of any kind, express or implied, including but not limited to the implied warranties of merchantability, fitness for a particular purpose.

The Publisher and Editor shall not be liable whatsoever...

Made with ❤ on the BookLeaf Publishing Platform
www.bookleafpub.in
www.bookleafpub.com

Dedication

To the ones who loved with their entire soul,
who believed in forever, even when forever walked
away.
To the fools who saw a Goddess in a mortal,
who kissed the ground she walked on,
who would have bled just to keep her warm.
To the ones who were shattered and still whispered, "I
love you."
To the ones who stood in the wreckage of their own
hearts
and still chose to smile.

This is for you—
the true lovers, the devastated lovers,
the ones who lost, the ones who still wait,
the ones who would do it all over again.

And to the betrayers—
read carefully. You may find yourselves in these pages.

Preface

Love is a myth until it isn't. Madness is a stranger until it becomes the only companion that stays. What begins as a dream—soft, golden, infinite—soon unravels into obsession, betrayal, and ruin.

But this is no ordinary tale of love and heartbreak. **This is something even the Gods did not dare to imagine—** a story carved into poetry, a journey unraveling verse by verse, emotion by emotion. A love so deep, it defies reason. A betrayal so cruel, it shatters the soul. A devotion so reckless, it cannot be undone.

These 21 poems are not just words. **They are echoes of a life once lived, a passion that burned too bright, a descent into the abyss of longing and loss.** Each poem is a fragment of the same story, **stitched together like the broken pieces of a man who could never stop loving, even when love destroyed him.**

For eighteen poems, this is reality—raw, merciless, unfiltered. And then, in the last three, **fate fractures.** Three alternate endings, three possible destinies, yet none can undo the love that once was.

But there is one truth that remains unshaken—**betrayal demands retribution.** And so, at the very end, there is one final reckoning, a **bonus poem where the betrayer pays his due.**

This book does not offer comfort. It does not offer salvation. **It only promises to make you feel.**

Read at your own risk.

Sincerely,

Pranav Sood

Acknowledgements

To my father, Dr. M.P. Sood, the man who instilled in me the love of words and who showed me that poetry is not just ink on paper but the very pulse of a soul. You taught me that art is rebellion, that poetry is defiance, that words can burn, heal, and live forever. If I have ever written something worth remembering, it is because you made me believe that stories can outlive the ones who write them.

To my mother, Mrs. Bandana Sood, who shaped my voice before I even knew I had one worth hearing. From elocution contests to the written word, your encouragement built the foundation for every verse, every line, every breath of poetry I create.

To my wife, Ms. Swati Suneja, who stands beside me in silence and in storms, whose presence is both a sanctuary and a spark. You remind me that love is not always spoken—sometimes, it is simply understood.

To **Ms. Pankhuri Gupta,** a friend and guide who has helped me in the journey of writing this book by her insights, brainstorming sessions, and most importantly by being honest about the work.

To the poets before me, who dared to put their hearts on paper, who bled ink so the world could feel—your words have echoed through time and found a home in me.

To the lovers who loved recklessly, worshipped blindly, and broke spectacularly—this book exists because of you. Your devotion, your agony, your resilience have shaped these verses.

To the betrayers—whether you meant to or not—you **made this inevitable.**

To the ones who will read this and see themselves in every line, every wound, every whispered prayer—you **are the reason words like these will never die.**

And finally, to fate itself—thank you for proving, time and time again, that even the most divine love stories are never safe from the cruelty of reality.

This is for all of you.

May these words find you at the right time.

1. Whispers of an Unseen Goddess - A dream

She walks where the moonlight dares not tread,
A ghost of silk, a hymn unsaid.
Stars kneel in the hollow of her sigh,
Yet she is mist—I cannot find her eye.

I feel her breath in the hush of the sea,
A phantom touch that unravels me.
She carves her name in the marrow of air,
Yet when I reach, there's nothing there.

She dances in embers, in echoes, in rain,
A deity spun from longing and pain.
My hands are altars, my lips are prayers,
But she is a shadow—vanishing stairs.

Oh, if time were mercy, if fate were kind,
Would she step from the fog, unchain my mind?
Or is she the curse I was born to adore,
A love unbirthed—forever lore?

2. And Then, She Happened - First Sighting

The air trembled—
not with sound, but with something deeper,
as if the earth had whispered a secret to the stars.

And then, she happened.

She walked, and gravity betrayed itself,
pulling me towards the orbit of her steps.
Light obeyed her, folding around her form
like a worshiper bowing to its Goddess.

She did not see me—
but I saw nothing else.

The world was a dull, forgotten thing,
a backdrop to the cathedral of her existence.
The wind carried the scent of her passing,
a cruel mercy, enough to ruin, never to have.

My lungs burned with a name they did not know,
a prayer forming for a deity unknown.

I had seen beauty before,
but never like this—
a beauty that unraveled me,
a beauty that made me less and made her everything.

3. The Shape of her -   A Goddess..

Her eyes, two eclipses swallowing light,
her lips, the edge where sinners ignite.

She moves like poetry written by fire,
a hymn of ruin, a whispered desire.

The sun envies the gold in her hair,
midnight itself is trapped in her stare.

No sculptor, no God, no dream could design
a creature so cruelly, divinely aligned.

She walks with the weight of a thousand stars,
a universe bending, unraveling in scars.

Her voice is a prophecy sung in the rain,
a melody crafted from pleasure and pain.

She is art without mercy, beauty untamed,

a story unfinished, yet already named.

She does not know she is worshiped in prayer,
does not see how the world holds its breath in her stare.

To her, I am silence—a shadow at best,
but she is the moon that eclipses my chest.

4. A Thousand Steps Away or Near

I see her, I know her, yet fear the air,
my feet are bound, my tongue is bare.
What is a mortal to say to a queen,
when even silence would dare not demean?

A thousand steps, a world apart,
and yet she already owns my heart.
I try to move, but time holds me still,
a prisoner to beauty, a slave to my will.

She laughs, and it breaks through the evening sky,
a sound too soft for a world so dry.
The Gods must have spent a lifetime in thought,
crafting a creature so flawlessly wrought.

My chest is a battlefield, my mind a war,
should I step forward, should I want more?
Yet what is longing but exquisite despair,
watching divinity... unaware?

5. The First Hello

A chance, a breath, a moment in time,
a hello that rang like a holy chime.

She smiled, and the night was erased,
her voice, a sound the heavens embraced.

In that moment, the world was just us,
and I, a disciple, undone by her trust.

Her lips curved, the birth of a star,
and suddenly galaxies weren't so far.

The world became quiet, the earth stood still,
her words wrapped around me, bending my will.

I had never known that sound had shape,
that syllables could imprison, that letters could drape.

She spoke my name, and I was unmade,
a man no longer, but something frayed.

If this was the start, let time never end,
let me drown in the space where syllables bend.

6. Falling Into the Abyss of Love

We spoke, we laughed, we breathed the same air,
and love, like a fever, grew unaware.
She held my hand, the cosmos shifted,
my soul surrendered, my spirit lifted.

To love her was not a choice nor a crime,
it was fate, it was death, it was reason and rhyme.
Her touch was a scripture my hands longed to trace,
a sacred design carved into space.

We chased the dawn, defied the clock,
and I learned that silence had ways to talk.
She wore the night in strands of black lace,
a queen, a tempest, unshaken in grace.

Yet love was a sickness I did not fight,
a feverish madness, a beautiful blight.
If loving her meant losing my mind,
then let me unravel, let fate stay blind.

7. The Proposal

With trembling hands and a heart untamed,
I knelt in devotion, whispering her name.
A box in my palm, a promise inside,
a question that quivered, too sacred to hide.

The stars held their breath, the moon cast its spell,
and time itself stumbled, unable to tell—
would she say yes, would fate align,
or was love just a flicker, a passing design?

Her eyes spilled galaxies, bright and unchained,
her lips curved in wonder, her heartbeat remained.
And when she spoke, the world came alive,
a single word, a vow to survive.

Yes—like a hymn, like the birth of the sun,
a new world beginning, a war finally won.
The universe shifted, the cosmos withdrew,
and love, undying, was finally true.

8. A Fire That Devours - Flames of Love

Our love was a flame, reckless and wild,
burning through caution, unholy, defiled.

She led me to places where reason would break,
where lust and devotion would fever and ache.

Her hands carved sin in the skin of my chest,
her mouth wrote gospel, my body confessed.

She was the altar, the priestess, the knife,
and I was the prayer surrendering life.

There was no ceiling, no ground, no air,
only her nails and teeth everywhere.

She called me by name like a spell torn apart,
and I answered in shudders, in gasps, in sparks.

The night bled soft as her thighs held tight,

pleasure and ruin in sacred delight.

No heaven, no hell—only this, only her,
a rapture too violent for angels to bear.

She was the sin I would never repent,
the prayer that would never relent.

If love was salvation, then let it be damned,
for I was baptized beneath her hands.

9. Future - In our hands

We spoke of a house with windows so wide,
where morning would kiss the dreams we confide.

A child with her laughter, a garden in bloom,
a life spun from whispers, dissolving all gloom.

She traced the stars on the back of my hand,
calling them maps to the world we had planned.

A dress she would wear, white as the tide,
my trembling hands lifting her veil aside.

She painted the years with colors so bright,
soft days of laughter, fierce love in the night.

A dog by the fire, our names on the gate,
a world of tomorrows sculpted by fate.

Yet fate is a tempest, a cruel shifting tide,
what is built in dreams, real life can divide.

But in that moment, we crafted our land,
and held the whole future within our hands

10. Whispers of Absence

The wind still carries her laughter home,
yet something in its echo feels alone.
Her touch still lingers like a holy psalm,
but somewhere, somehow, it's lost its calm.

She kisses me, yet something is amiss,
like a ghost lingers beneath her kiss.
Her hands still trace the lines of my skin,
but they move like someone searching within.

I tell myself, *No, she is mine,*
A Goddess does not wane, does not decline.
Yet the stars that once followed where she led
now flicker like lanterns mourning the dead.

She smiles, and I swear it's the same,
but the warmth has lessened inside the flame.
She calls me love, she calls me dear,
but something in her voice feels **insincere**.

And yet, I kneel, a fool in prayer,
worshiping a love that's thinning in air.
For even if absence takes its place,
I will still call her divine, still crave her grace.

11. A Stranger in Her Arms

Her body is warm, yet colder than before,
wrapped in my arms, yet distant to the core.
Her lips meet mine, but something resists,
as if love hesitates before it exists.

The nights stretch long in a hollow embrace,
her heartbeat a whisper I struggle to trace.
She turns to me, yet her eyes look through,
searching for something she already knew.

I tell myself, *Love does not fade,*
A Goddess remains, she cannot degrade.
But shadows grow where certainty stood,
where once was fire, now lies wood.

She laughs, but it doesn't belong to me,
a melody played in another key.
Her hands still wander, but only in part,
as if seeking an exit, a door from my heart.

Yet still, I kiss her, still I believe,
for Gods do not falter, and love does not leave.

18

12. The Lie I Chose to Believe

A glance too long, a touch too light,
a whisper stolen in the dying night.
His name on her lips, soft as a prayer,
and yet, I tell myself *nothing is there.*

They laugh in a way I've never heard,
a language unspoken, a silent word.
His hand lingers a moment too much,
fingertips grazing where mine once touched.

But she turns to me, and smiles just the same,
calls me *love*, calls me *by name.*
And though something in her voice sounds thin,
I bury the doubt, refuse to begin.

For a Goddess does not deceive, does not stray,
a Goddess does not take love away.
If I have worshiped, if I have prayed,
how could she let faith decay?

So I cast the shadow from my mind,
paint over cracks, pretend I'm blind.
For even if she slips, even if she sways,
I will believe her, till my dying days.

13. The Moment I Died

I was not searching, yet I found.
Fate, cruel and laughing, dragged me down.
A door left open, a thread undone,
a love that once burned, now eclipsed by the sun.

His voice, a murmur tangled in silk,
her sigh, a song tainted with guilt.
Fingers in hair that I used to own,
lips on skin where my worship was sewn.

I called her name, and she turned too slow,
guilt painted in shades only the damned would know.
His hands retreated, hers stayed still,
a queen uncrowned, a king left to kill.

The world did not end, yet nothing remained,
only silence, only shame.
She spoke, but words had lost their weight,
as if even language had learned to betray.

I stood, I watched, I did not break—
for Gods do not bleed, and men do not wake.
But something left me in that room,
a ghost, a whisper, a love entombed.

I walked away, yet I did not leave.
I breathed, but I did not breathe.

For I had died before their eyes,
and neither of them dared to grieve.

14. A Love that Refuses to Rot

I should burn her name from my lips,
rip the ghost of her from my ribs.

I should curse her, abandon my prayer,
but even in ruin, she lingers there.

I wake to her laughter carved in my chest,
the taste of her sin still fresh on my breath.
Like poison that soothes, like fire that heals,
I drink from the cup that shattered my shield.

They whisper, they pity, they tell me to run,
as if love were a battle that could be won.
But I do not seek freedom, I do not seek peace,
I kneel in the wreckage and beg for release.

For love does not die—it festers, it feeds,
it burrows in places too hollow to bleed.
And though she has left me, though she has strayed,

I love her more with each step away.

Her betrayal, a dagger; her absence, a crown,
yet still, I kneel, still, I bow.

For Gods may be cruel, may shatter and rot,
but devotion like mine cannot be forgot.
She is the sickness, and I am the host.
She is the haunting, and I am the ghost.

And even in death, I will call her divine,
for what is a God, if not worshiped in crime?

15. A God Does Not Beg - Yet I Do!

I watch her from across the street,
where love was buried, yet my heart still beats.
She laughs in the arms of the man I called friend,
as if she never vowed this would never end.

She does not flinch, does not turn,
does not feel my gaze as I burn.
Does she know that I stand in the rain for hours,
watching the ghost of what once was ours?

I could break them—I should.
I could crush them—I would.

But when her eyes meet mine, I become undone,
for even in ruin, she is still the sun.

So I write to her in letters she'll never read,
spilling devotion like open wounds that bleed.
"Come back," I scrawl, then scratch it away,

for Gods do not return, and I am only prey.

"I should hate you," I ink in the dark,
but hate is a language I cannot start.
For love is a beast that does not die,
it lingers, it festers, it rots inside.

So I fold my words into silence instead,
and whisper my prayers to the sheets of my bed.

A God does not beg, yet here I remain—
a sinner, a servant, still mouthing her name.

16. A Martyr of Love.

I placed her hands in his, steady and sure,
a final act of love—painful, pure.

I smiled through wounds that bled like the sky,
whispered, *"Take care of her,"* then whispered goodbye.

They never saw the tremor inside,
the way my ribs collapsed and died.
They never heard the silent screams
of a man who drowned inside his dreams.

I watched from afar as their love took flight,
stood in the dark while they bathed in the light.
I taught him the ways she loved to be held,
how to calm her storms when her oceans swelled.

And when I knew she was safe, she was whole,
I carved out my heart and buried my soul.

I left without footprints, without a trace,

a name forgotten, an erased face.
Perhaps love is not meant to be owned,
but given, set free, a ghost overthrown.

And though I am nothing, I still softly pray—
that she wakes up happy, at least once, each day.

And when I am certain you need me no more,
I step through the night and close the door.

No notes, no whispers, no trace to find,
just an echo, a breath, a love left behind.
You will wake to a world unstained by me,
and I will dissolve—like mist in the sea.

17. The Art of Letting Go (But Never Really)

I burned your name in a fire last night,
watched the embers rise like birds in flight.

I whispered, "Be free," as the ashes swayed,
but love is a ghost that never obeys.

I kissed strangers with empty lips,
held their hands but felt your fingertips.

I traced new skin, but under the light,
every touch still felt like yours in the night.

I told myself love was a trick of the mind,
a fever, a sickness, a dream left behind.

But dreams do not vanish—they sleep in the cracks,
waiting for silence to pull them back.

I let you go in a thousand ways,

in fire, in whiskey, in long summer days.

But no matter how far, no matter the show,
the art of letting go is just letting you know—
I never will.

18. A Man Who Will Never Die, Yet Never Live

Once, I traced galaxies on your skin,
whispered eternity beneath your chin.
Once, my hands carved futures in air,
we built a kingdom—love was the heir.

Once, I dreamed of children with your eyes,
of wedding bells beneath quiet skies.
Once, your voice was the language of God,
now it's the hymn to which I rot.

I should hate you—I pray to hate you,
but love is a wound that refuses to fade.
I drink from the venom, I beg for the poison,
but even ruin bows where your shadow is laid.

I am not dead, nor am I alive,
I walk, I breathe, I curse, I writhe.
I smile where the world demands I must,
but my ribs are coffins filled with dust.

I wander through days that have lost their weight,
pretending that fate is not laughing at fate.
That I do not see you in every street,
that my heart does not crawl to your feet.

Tell me—do you sleep without ghosts in your bed?
Do my lips ever haunt the back of your head?
Or am I the only one damned to remain,
a love-stricken corpse that answers to pain?

For some men die and are free to decay,
but I am cursed to stay.
To love, to ache, to wither, to crawl,
to live like a man who never lived at all

19. Alternate Ending 1: She Returns (Its Time for Revenge)

She came back like a whisper in the night,
a shadow trembling under the pale streetlight.
Barefoot, breathless, soaked in regret,
but love is not mercy—love never forgets.

"I was wrong," she wept, voice cracked in sin,
"I searched the world, but it led me back to him."

She clutched my hands, knelt in disgrace,
as if begging absolution from a long-dead face.
Did she think love was a door left ajar?
That she could return after breaking my heart?

Did she think Gods forgive when their temples fall?
Did she forget I am no man at all?

My fingers brushed against her shaking frame,

soft as a whisper, cruel as a flame.
"You were my Goddess," I said with a sigh,
"but even deities bleed before they die."

She reached for my lips, pleading, divine,
but my mouth was a grave where love went to die.
I kissed her like venom, like sins left unsaid,
let her drown in the ghosts of the love she had fled.

Then I pulled her close, tangled in doom,
whispered revenge as I breathed in her perfume.
I loved her once, and love turned to spite,
so let her burn in this hell of the night.

She wanted redemption, she wanted release,
but I was the storm that would never make peace.
If she could betray, then so could I—
so I worshiped her body, but cursed her inside.

And when the dawn came, when the madness withdrew,
I left her alone, broken, untrue.
For the wrath of a devoted man runs deep,
and not all betrayals are buried in sleep.

20. Alternate Ending 2: She Returns (Pure Redemption)

She came back with the autumn wind,
soft as a prayer, lost, paper-thin.
Her eyes held storms she could not contain,
and her lips trembled with unspoken pain.

"I was a fool," she whispered, voice barely whole,
"I lost myself, and I lost my soul."

Tears traced rivers down her golden face,
a Goddess unthroned, begging for grace.

I stood in silence, torn and unchained,
years of love and years of pain.
Could I forgive? Could I believe?
Was love a wound, or could it still breathe?

She fell to her knees, hands over mine,
*"I have nothing left—just one last sign.
If love was real, if love was true,*

then even now, it must lead me to you."

And in that moment, the past was erased,
not forgotten, but lovingly faced.
I pulled her close, no anger, no war,
just two broken hearts wanting no more.

She did not beg, and I did not speak,
we simply stood, fragile and weak.
For love is not perfect, nor always wise,
but sometimes, it finds a way to rise.

And so we rose, from ruin, from dust,
not Gods, not fools—just two who still trust.

21. Alternate Ending 3: She Cannot Return   (She Was Never Real)

They whispered it first, in passing.
Friends, strangers—concern in their eyes,
hesitation in their words.
"She never existed."
I laughed. Dismissed it.

How could they deny what I had held?
How could they erase the fire that burned through me,
the hands that mapped my ruin, the lips that spoke my
name
as if it was sacred?

But the whispers grew.
"There was never a girl."
"You were always alone."
"Check your photos. Read your texts. She's not there."
And then—**I did.**

My hands trembled as I scrolled through my phone,
through the hundreds of messages I knew we had
shared.
But there was nothing.
No calls. No pictures. No traces.

Only me, sending words into an abyss,
whispering love to a ghost.
The bed was too empty.
The perfume on my pillow—vanished.

The letters I swore she wrote—blank pages staring back.
But I **remembered—I felt** her.
She was fire and silk, cruelty and grace.
She was the storm I drowned in.

How could she not be real?
I ran through the streets, screaming her name,
but no one turned. No one **knew** her.

A cold hand gripped my throat. **Had I dreamed her?**
Had I carved her from my own longing?
Had my love been a mirage so perfect,
even reality bowed to it?

Or was this the punishment of devotion—

to love so deeply, so recklessly,
that the universe itself erased her
to break me completely?

And if she was never real...
Then who had ruined me?

22. The Judas Who Called Me Brother

He sat there, laughing.
Drinking from my glass.
Smiling with **my Goddess** on his lap.
Hands where my hands used to be.

Lips where my lips used to belong.
"Brother," he had once called me,
a word that now tasted like bile, like rot,
like a lie so deep it deserved its own grave.

Did he think I would break?
Did he think I would weep?
No, brother, no. **I do not mourn traitors.**
I bury them.

I walked towards him, slow, deliberate—
a ghost in the body of a man,
a storm dressed in skin.
He smirked. **That was his first mistake.**

"Still bitter?" he asked.
And oh, if only he knew.
I grabbed his wrist—**hard.**

The same wrist that once clasped mine in brotherhood.
The same wrist that now reeked of my Goddess.
I twisted it until **bone snapped like a lover's whisper.**
He screamed. **Music to my ears.**

The bar fell silent, eyes wide, breaths held—
but **no one moved.**
They knew.
They **knew.**
"She was never yours," he spat through clenched teeth.
"She chose me."
Wrong answer.

I slammed his face into the table.
Glass shattered, blood spilled, teeth clattered like dice
rolling for fate.
He groaned, his body slumping—but I wasn't done.
I wanted him to **taste betrayal the way I did.**

So I leaned in, whispering where only he could hear:
"You think you won? You think you took her?"
I chuckled.
"You took her? Claimed her? Called her yours?

41

Brother, I was inside her more nights
than you will spend in your entire life.
She moaned my name like a prayer you'll never hear,
whispered sins into my ear that you'll never know.
Every inch of her? Marked by me.
Every echo of her pleasure? Taught by me.
You're living in my shadow, tasting what I left behind—
and you will never, ever be enough."

His swollen eyes twitched. Confusion. Fear.
Good. Let it **sink in.**

Let him wonder if she ever truly moaned for him,
or if every gasp was just an echo of me.
Let him rot in the same madness that devoured me,
knowing he was never her first choice—
just a shadow cast by a love that burned too bright.
I walked away, leaving him in a pool of his own blood.
Not dead.

No—**death would be mercy.**
And I am no longer merciful.

www.ingramcontent.com/pod-product-compliance
Lightning Source LLC
Chambersburg PA
CBHW052303150726

47996CB00020B/2458

This is not just poetry—it's a reckoning.
A love so divine it felt like worship.
A betrayal so cruel it tasted like blood.
A devotion so blind it teetered between madness and martyrdom.
Told through 21 gut-wrenching poems, this book is not just about heartbreak—it's about the addiction to pain, the beauty in destruction, and the inescapable hunger for the one who ruined you.
Lovers will relate. Betrayers will flinch. And the broken will bleed all over again.
Enter this story at your own risk. You've been warned.
(Bonus poem included: an unfiltered, brutal reckoning for the one who broke the bro-code.)

ABOUT THE AUTHOR

Pranav Sood is an award-winning lawyer, honoured at the LexTalk World Global Legal & IP Conference in Singapore as the Emerging Independent Practitioner of the Year. Featured in Passion Vista Magazine's Global Game Changers 2024 edition, he's known for his sharp legal acumen and unwavering pursuit of justice.

But beyond the courtroom, Pranav is a poet — one who bends words until they break, he crafts poetry that is raw, rebellious, and unapologetically intense. This book is a reflection of his duality: the strategist and the storyteller, the fighter and the feeler.

India | USA | UK

9789369538591

Just Two Years

Reflections of Young Motherhood

C. M. Palmer